I ♥ UNICORNS

Buster Books

Illustrated
by Jessie Eckel

Edited by Imogen Williams
Designed by Derrian Bradder

First published in Great Britain in 2018 by Buster Books, an imprint of
Michael O'Mara Books Limited, 9 Lion Yard, Tremadoc Road, London SW4 7NQ

With additional material adapted from www.shutterstock.com

W www.mombooks.com/buster   f Buster Books   🐦 @BusterBooks

ISBN: 978-1-78055-552-2

4 6 8 10 9 7 5

This book was printed in July 2018 by
Gutenberg Press Ltd, Gudja Road,
Tarxien GXQ 2902, Malta.

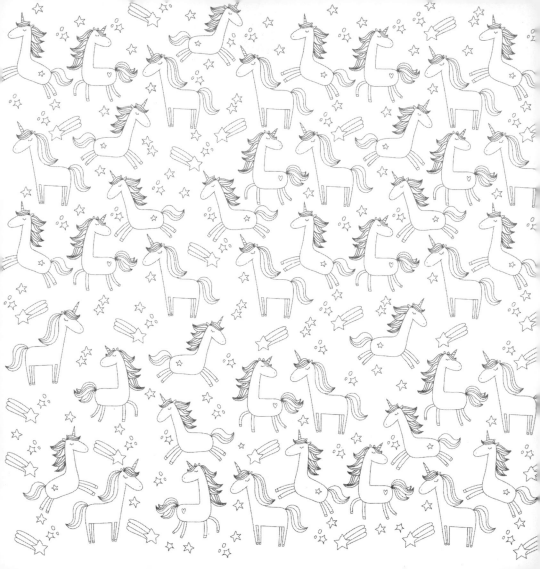

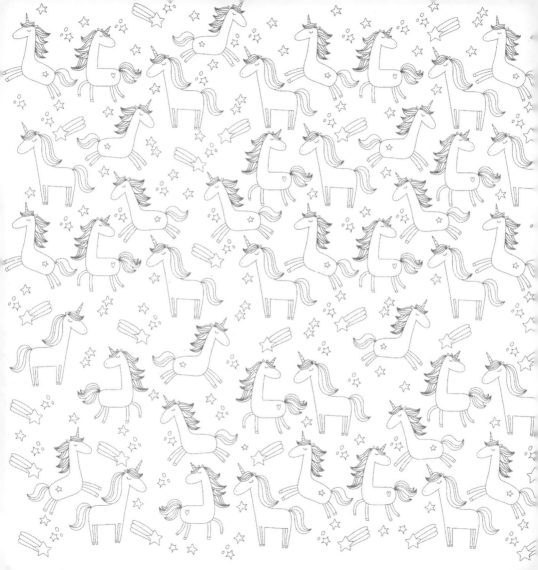